HAYDN

SIX SONATINAS FOR THE PIANO

EDITED BY WILLARD A. PALMER

ORIGIN

No autographs of the compositions now known as the *SIX SONATINAS* of Franz Joseph Haydn have survived. All of these works, however, are recognized as authentic compositions of Haydn and are listed in the Hoboken catalogue of Haydn's complete works under Group XVI, with the numbers 4, 7, 8, 9, 10 and 11. Only Nos. 10 and 11 were published during Haydn's lifetime, and No. 10 was first attributed to Haydn's pupil, Ignaz Pleyel. These works have been handed down in the form of manuscript copies made by pupils of Haydn or by his copyists. None originally bore the title Sonatina. Hoboken Nos. 4, 7 and 8 each bear the title *Divertimento for Clavicembalo Solo;* Nos. 9, 10 and 11 were each called *Sonata for Clavicembalo Solo.* Because of the form and brevity of these compositions, they may accurately be called Sonatinas. All were composed before 1768, and although they were conceived for the harpsichord, the first publication by J. Cooper, c. 1790, specified "harpsichord or pianoforte." They are well suited to the piano and contain much that is the essence of the Haydn style.

In the present edition, the sonatinas are arranged in approximate order of difficulty rather than according to number. The original text, in dark print, is taken from the earliest available sources. Editorial suggestions are in lighter print.

ORNAMENTATION

Haydn once said, "Whoever knows me thoroughly must discover that I owe a great deal to Emanuel Bach, that I understood him and studied him diligently. Emanuel Bach once complimented me on this fact himself."

Haydn is known to have recommended Carl Philipp Emanuel Bach's *ESSAY ON THE TRUE ART OF PLAYING KEYBOARD INSTRUMENTS* to his young friend, Mozart. He also expressed admiration for Mozart's father's famous method of violin playing, which is in substantive agreement with C.P.E. Bach's *ESSAY* regarding the performance of ornaments.

The general rule that all ornaments begin on the beat and the practice of starting all trills on the upper note must certainly be applied to the music of Haydn.

The following discussion deals only with those ornaments used in the *SIX SONATINAS*.

Cover art: A detail from a portrait of Haydn
by *John Hoppner (English, 1758–1810)*
Oil on canvas, 1791
The Royal Collection
©*1993 Her Majesty Queen Elizabeth II*

1.   THE SINGLE APPOGGIATURA

C.P.E. Bach probably originated the practice of showing the duration of the small note by using note values corresponding to the true length of the note. Thus the small notes were written as small quarters, eighths, sixteenths, etc., and this value was subtracted from the following note. Haydn generally followed this practice, particularly in the writing of the single appoggiatura. The general rules set forth by C.P.E. Bach and other writers of the period state:

  a. The appoggiatura is played *on the beat.*

  b. The appoggiatura takes half the time value of the following note, except when followed by a dotted note. It then usually takes two-thirds of the value of the note.

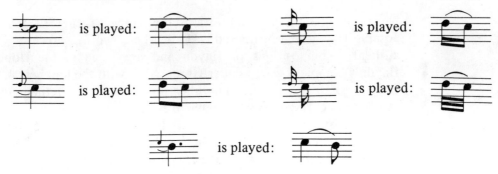

2.   THE DOUBLE APPOGGIATURA

The double appoggiatura appears in the *Sonatinas* only in the form of two small notes ascending to the principal note. When used in this fashion, the ornament becomes a *schleifer* or *slide* and is played as quickly as possible, regardless of the written value of the notes. The first of the two small notes must be played *on the beat.*

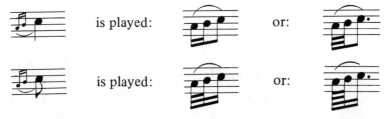

3.   THE MORDENT

In his *ESSAY,* C.P.E. Bach states, "The mordent is an essential ornament which connects notes, fills them out, and makes them brilliant." In Haydn's music, the function is usually to contribute brilliance. The mordent should be played rapidly, coming to rest on the principal note as quickly as possible. The Latin origin of the word, the verb "mordere" (to bite), suggests the incisive quality appropriate to the proper performance.

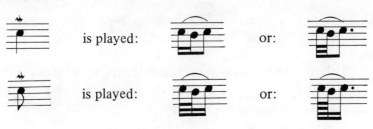

4.   THE TURN ∽

In his *ESSAY*, C.P.E. Bach remarks that "the turn is almost always performed rapidly."

When the turn appears over the note, it is played as follows:

When the turn appears after the note, the principal note is sounded before the turn is played.

In a letter to his publisher, Haydn wrote, "In the case of dotted notes the turn must stand over the dot. Leave plenty of space between the notes to make this clear." (In Haydn's time the dot was not placed closely after the note, but further to the right to show the point of the lengthening of the note: ♩ ⋅ ♪)

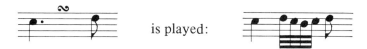

5.   THE TRILL *tr*

Haydn uses the symbol *tr* to indicate a long or short trill. All trills begin on the upper auxiliary. In C.P.E. Bach's *ESSAY*, he says of the trill, "It always begins on the tone above the principal note." This fact is also emphasized by Couperin, Rameau, Marpurg, Türk, Quantz, Leopold Mozart, and other 18th century writers of music instruction books and treatises on ornamentation.

The trill often comes to rest on the principal note, but it may consume the entire value of the note.

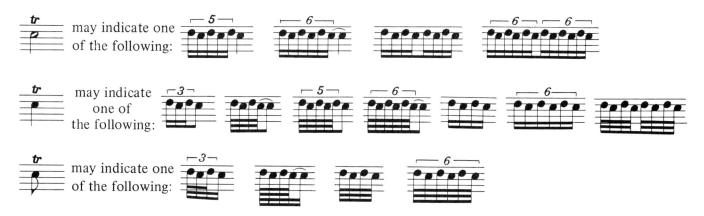

The number of repercussions in any trill depends upon the tempo of the selection as well as the skill and taste of the performer.

6.   THE TRILL WITH TERMINATION

Many short trills and almost all long trills are played with a termination or suffix consisting of two notes; the note just below the principal note (a half or whole step lower) followed by the principal note.

The termination is sometimes written out in full. When any trill is followed by a written termination, the trill consumes the full value of its principal note. The notes of the trill and the termination are performed at the same speed.

The trill with termination is especially appropriate when the note following the trill is a whole step or half step higher than the principal note of the trill. In such a case, the termination is effective, even with short trills.

7. THE PREPARED TRILL

In this ornament, the appoggiatura serves as the first note of the trill, which is prolonged for the written value of the appoggiatura.

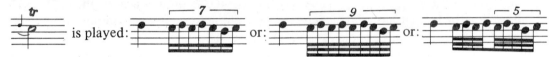

THE SIMPLIFICATION OF TRILLS

Because of the lighter action of the harpsichord, the trill was more easily performed on that instrument than on the piano. In the *SIX SONATINAS,* there are several trills that might require simplification for some students.

In Haydn's time the trill was primarily a harmonic ornament, serving the same harmonic function as the descending appoggiatura. For this reason an appoggiatura

is a better substitute for a short trill than the so-called "inverted mordent"

(schneller) . A possible exception will be found in the *Sonatina in F Major*

on page 13 (see footnote a).

The best substitute for a short trill with termination is a turn. Since the turn begins on the upper auxiliary, it satisfies the harmonic requirement of an upper-note trill. Since it ends the same as a trill with termination, the two ornaments lead to the following note in an identical manner. In his *ESSAY,* C.P.E. Bach says of the turn, "If one considers that this ornament represents, in a shortened form, an ordinary trill with termination, one can get some idea of its proper use."

THE ADDITION OF ORNAMENTS

In Haydn's day it was customary for performers to add ornaments at their own discretion; a performer who played only the written text was likely to be considered dull and unimaginative. C.P.E. Bach's *ESSAY* goes into considerable detail concerning musical situations in which certain ornaments are appropriate, although he remarks that "it is best for composers to specify the proper ornaments unmistakably rather than to leave their selection to the whims of tasteless performers." A few composers tried carefully to make their wishes known by writing the indication for ornaments more consistently than others, but almost all of them, including Haydn, expected the performer to take the addition of certain ornaments for granted.

A trill at a cadence was considered a matter of course, and although some of them were indicated, many were not.

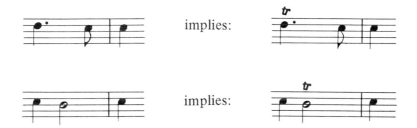

In the second example, the trill sounds best with a suffix, because it is followed by the note one diatonic step higher. The trill must begin on the upper note, which may either be tied to the preceding note or played again, as the taste of the performer may dictate.

Another occasion calling for the addition of ornaments is in the recurrence of thematic material that has been ornamented in its first appearance. In such a case, the composer sometimes omitted the ornaments in subsequent appearances of the theme because their use was obvious.

This editor does not believe, however, that the converse is true. An ornament used only in a later appearance of a theme does not necessarily have to be used the first time the theme occurs. In such cases the ornament might be part of a development of the theme.

HAYDN'S USE OF THE SLUR

In the *SIX SONATINAS*, only a few slurs are indicated by Haydn. Like many composers who wrote primarily for orchestra and for string ensembles, Haydn wrote slurs as if they were written to indicate the bowing for stringed instruments. On stringed instruments, groups of notes under one slur are taken in one direction of the bow. Often the direction of the bow is changed, not to make a break in the legato, but to place a slight stress or emphasis on the first note played in the new direction.

When Haydn writes

he certainly does not intend to indicate a break between the 1st and 2nd counts of either measure. He does intend to imply a bit of emphasis on the notes falling on each beat of both measures. This same phrasing might be indicated for the piano as follows:

This principle must be borne in mind in playing this music, particularly in playing the slurs taken from the original sources, which are indicated in the present edition in heavy print.

DYNAMICS

No dynamics are indicated in the early sources of the *SIX SONATINAS*. At the time they were composed, the most commonly used dynamic device was the antiphonal or "echo" effect. Passages first played forte were repeated softly. D.G. Türk, in his *KLAVIERSCHULE* (1789), wrote that every repeat of a period should be played softly unless it were first played softly, in which case it should be played forte on its repetition. C.P.E. Bach, in his *ESSAY,* wrote, "Entire passages. . . . may first be marked forte and, later, piano. This is a customary procedure with both repetitions and sequences, particularly when the accompaniment is modified." Although this device is highly compatible with music of this period, the fact is that it will not always work convincingly. When the echo effect does work, it can still become tiresome if indulged in too frequently in the same selection. The student will find ample opportunity to experiment with echo effects in the *SIX SONATINAS,* which abound in repeated motives, phrases and sections.

Other effects, mentioned by Leopold Mozart and other writers of Haydn's time, are the crescendo on the ascending melodic line, the diminuendo on the descending line, the emphasis on high notes of lively passages and stress on the longest notes of the melodic line. Such effects are so naturally a part of musical expression that they need not always be marked; doing so might lead some students to exaggerate them.

In the present edition, the dynamics in lighter print should be regarded as mere suggestions, and the student should be encouraged to discover other effects more pleasing to him.

ACKNOWLEDGMENTS

I would like to express my thanks to Irving Chasnov and Morton Manus of Alfred Music Company for the meticulous care with which they helped to prepare this edition. I also wish to thank Judith Simon Linder for her valuable assistance in the research necessary for the realization of this edition, and for her help in preparing the manuscript.

Six Sonatinas, Opus 36

by Franz Joseph Haydn

Willard A. Palmer, Editor

THEMATIC INDEX

SONATINA IN G MAJOR

Allegro M.M. ♩ = 80 – 84 (♪ = 160 – 168)

ⓐ A *turn* may be substituted. See THE SIMPLIFICATION OF TRILLS on page 5.

ⓑ A *turn* may be substituted for the *trill*.

Pulse: 123, 123, 123

no staccato

Menuet M.M. ♩ = 100–104

ⓐ See the discussion of the *slur*, on pages 6 and 7.

ⓑ The measure may also be played:

ⓐ This *trill* and the following one may be played with more repercussions.

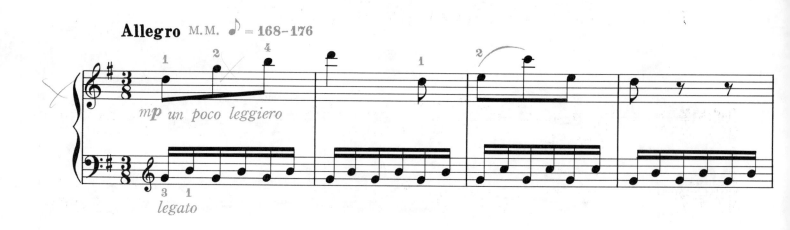

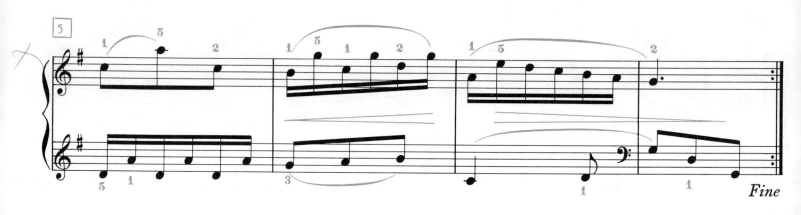

SONATINA IN F MAJOR

H.XVI No. 9

ⓐ   At a fast tempo, the *schneller* may be acceptable here as a substitute for the trill:

This solution is recommended in Ignaz Pleyel's *Methode pour le Pianoforte* (c. 1800), when a trill occurs in a rapid, descending passage. The same solution is allowed in Muzio Clementi's *Introduction to the Art of Playing on the Pianoforte* (c. 1803), when it is necessary to preserve a legato with the note preceding the trill.

ⓑ The notes in this measure, taken from the first edition, are certainly correct.

Most editions have the following:

ⓒ See ⓐ on page 13.

Menuet M.M. ♩ = 108~116

ⓐ Some editors add a *trill* here, corresponding to the *trill* in measure 5.

ⓑ A *trill* may be added here, played:

ⓒ This realization applies a rule given by Joachim Quantz: "When a rest follows a note, the appoggiatura receives the value of the note, and the note the value of the rest."

ⓓ Some editors add a *trill* here and in measure 22, corresponding to the *trill* in the 5th measure.

ⓔ Each section of the Trio may be played *mf* the first time and softer the second time.

ⓕ See ⓒ on page 16.

ⓖ The *trill* at the cadence is not indicated in the early sources but should be added. See THE ADDITION OF ORNAMENTS on page 6.

Scherzo

SONATINA IN C MAJOR

H. XVI No. 7

ⓐ See footnote ⓒ on page 16.
ⓑ A *trill* at the cadence is desirable, if not too difficult:

Menuet da Capo

ⓒ A *trill* at the cadence is desirable:

Finale

Allegro M.M. ♪ =152−168

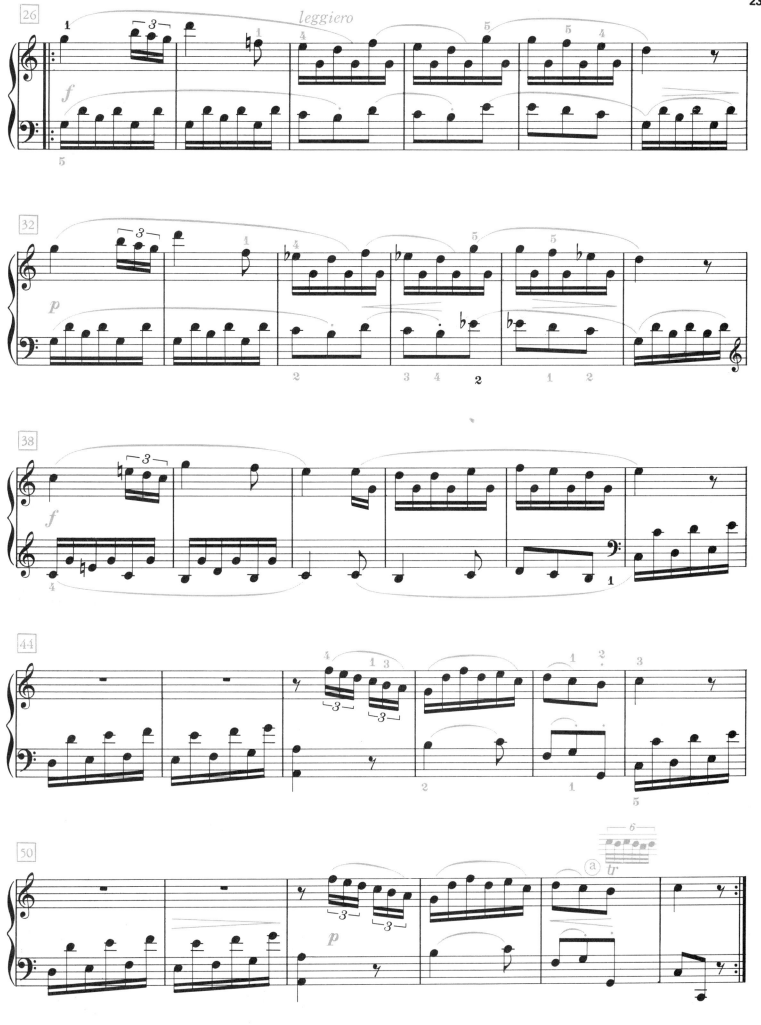

ⓐ A *turn* may be substituted for the *trill*. See THE SIMPLIFICATION OF TRILLS on page 5.

SONATINA IN G MAJOR

H.XVI No. 11

D. C. al Fine

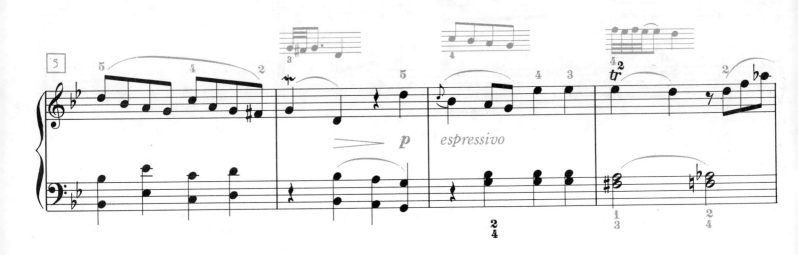

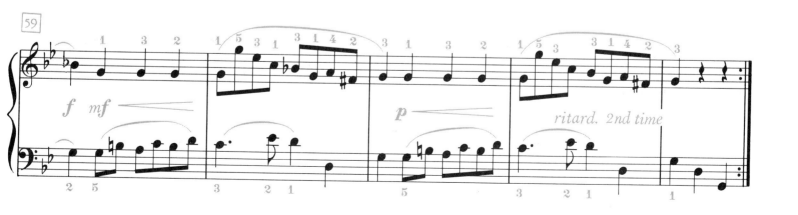

Menuet

Menuet D.C.

Play this one

SONATINA IN D MAJOR

H. XVI No. 4

Allegro M.M. ♩=80-84 (♪=160-168)   2/27/13

ⓐ In other editions, this *turn* stands directly over the first note. This is not in accordance with Haydn's instructions to his publisher regarding the use of the *turn* with a dotted note. See page 4.

ⓑ The *trill* may be played: or

ⓒ At a fast tempo, a turn   may be substituted for the *trill*. See THE SIMPLIFICATION OF TRILLS on page 5.

ⓓ A *turn* may be substituted for the *trill*.

Menuet

M.M. ♩ = 100 – 108

ⓐ See ⓒ on page 16.

ⓑ The *trill* may be played:

Fine

Menuet da Capo

SONATINA IN C MAJOR

H. XVI No. 10

Moderato M.M. ♩ = 66–69 (♪ = 132–138)

ⓐ   See the discussion of the *slur* on page 6.

ⓑ   The realization follows Quantz's rule. See ⓒ on page 16. The rule is also applied in measures 25 and 42 of this movement.

ⓒ   A *turn* ♩♩♩♩ may be substituted for the *trill*. See THE SIMPLIFICATION OF TRILLS on page 5.

ⓓ A *turn* 𝄃𝄃 may be substituted for the *trill*.

Menuet

This sonatina was attributed to Haydn's pupil, I. Pleyel, in the first edition (J. Cooper, c. 1790). The Cooper edition includes an "accompaniment" for violin, and a surplus of ornaments. We have included only those ornaments found in earlier sources, except where mentioned in footnotes.

ⓐ The *prepared trill* is taken from the first edition. It may also be played as follows:

Menuet da Capo

ⓒ The realization follows a rule by Quantz. See ⓒ on page 16. The Cooper edition has no appoggiatura, but shows a turn (∾) over the quarter note C.

ⓐ These *trills* may be played with *terminations.* See the discussion on pages 4 and 5. The Cooper edition has a *turn* in measure 38 instead of a *trill,* but has *trills* in measures 41 and 44.

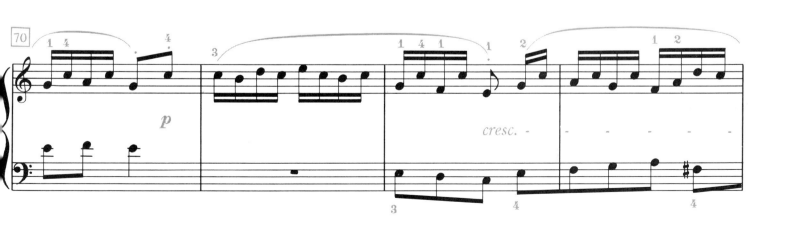

48

ⓑ Here the Cooper edition has **tr**